Soulful Southern Cooking

Favorite Southern Comfort Food Recipes

Louise Davidson

ISBN: 9781523638734

Printed in the United States

www.thecookbookpublisher.com

Contents

Introduction

If you are a fan of Southern food and hearty meals, this is the perfect recipe book to give your taste buds a delightful kick. After a long stressful day, one is lucky to come home to a peaceful house and a hearty home cooked meal. American Southern food is more than just a cuisine: it is a means of bringing people together. In fact, it is impossible to decide which meal is the most delicious. With its rich, wholesome flavors, American Southern food has a variety of dishes associated with comfort food.

From fried chicken to macaroni and cheese, the southern U.S. is home to some of the most unique foods and has a wide variety of flavors to offer. American Southern food has become integrated with the cultural identity of the South. Whether it is deep fried chicken or barbecued pork, American Southern food is extremely hard to resist.

Hop aboard the journey where we explore some of the best southern food flavors. Without any further wait, let's get started.

Appetizers

Corn Chowder

You just can't resist trying your hand at Corn Chowder. In fact, this hearty soup can carry a meal at the end of summer. With its rich corn and bacon, this creamy recipe is the perfect Southern Styled Corn Chowder.

Makes 10 to 12 Servings

Ingredients

4 ounces chopped bacon

½ cup celery, finely chopped

½ cup carrots, finely chopped

1 cup onions, finely chopped

2 tablespoons garlic, minced

¼ cup all-purpose flour

2 quarts chicken stock

1 ½ cups russet potatoes, cubed and peeled

1 cup heavy cream

5 cups kernel corn

¾ cup red bell peppers, finely chopped

1 tablespoon salt

¼ teaspoon cayenne pepper

Finely chopped parsley for garnishing

Directions

1. Place an 8 quart stockpot over medium heat and allow the bacon to cook until it is crispy. This should take about 5 minutes.
2. When the bacon is cooked, remove it to drain on a paper towel.
3. To the stockpot, add the onions, carrots, and celery and allow the mixture to cook, stirring occasionally, it until it is soft, about 5 minutes.
4. Add garlic, bell peppers, and corn to the pot and allow cook for 10 minutes, stirring often.
5. Sprinkle the flour over the vegetables, and stir constantly for 5 minutes. Slowly pour in the chicken stock, mixing to combine all the ingredients. You may use a whisk if necessary to break up the lumps if any have formed.
6. Add the potatoes and bring the mixture to a boil, and cook for at least 20 minutes, until the potatoes are fork tender.
7. Finally, add salt, cayenne pepper, and stir in the cream.
8. Garnish with some bacon and fresh parsley. Enjoy!

Hot Corn Dip

This spicy and cheesy corn dip with tortillas makes a perfect combination. Fall in love with this easy dip that takes less than five minutes to put together.

Makes 10 servings

Ingredients

2 cups corn kernel

½ cup diced onion

2 tablespoons mayonnaise

1 ½ tablespoons butter

1 clove garlic, minced

1-2 jalapenos, seeded and diced

¼ teaspoon seasoned salt

¾ cup sharp cheddar cheese, shredded

½ cup Monterey Jack Cheese, shredded

¼ teaspoon chili powder

4 tablespoons cream cheese

1 green onion, sliced

Tortilla chips for dipping

Cooking spray

Directions

1. Preheat oven to 375°F.
2. In a skillet, melt butter, and add corn, onion, and jalapeño. Sauté for 3 minutes.
3. Add garlic and continue to sauté for 1 to 2 more minutes.
4. Remove the mixture from heat and allow the mixture to cool for a few minutes before adding all the remaining ingredients. Stir to combine.
5. Transfer to a baking dish coated with cooking spray, and bake for 20 minutes, until the cheese bubbles.
6. Serve with tortilla chips for dipping.

Pinto Beans

Hearty, flavorful pinto beans make an excellent side dish and are good with just about everything. This Southern Style staple is sure to remind you of sunny afternoon barbecues. Sometimes, all you need is a good old hearty bowl of Pinto beans to fill you to the brim. The flourish of thyme and oregano adds an exotic aroma and taste.

Makes 8 to 10 servings

Ingredients

2 cups dried pinto beans

4 cups of chicken broth

¼ pound cooked ham, shredded

1 teaspoon black pepper

½ teaspoon thyme

2 teaspoons salt

½ teaspoon garlic powder

½ teaspoon dried oregano

¼ teaspoon chili powder

¼ teaspoon ground cumin

3 bay leaves

Directions

1. Soak the beans in water overnight, or for at least 6 to 8 hours

2. The following day, drain the beans and discard the water, and place the beans in a slow cooker with all the other ingredients.

3. Cook the mixture on low for 10 hours, or on high for 5 hours

4. After the mixture has finished cooking, take 2 cups of the bean soup and puree, using a food processor or blender.

5. Add the puree back to the beans, and cook on high for at least 30 minutes. This will thicken the soup.

6. Remove the beans from the slow cooker and serve.

Tip: serve the beans with freshly baked corn bread and fried potatoes.

Fried Shrimp

If you are in mood for some good old-fashioned fried shrimp, you will never believe how easy it is to make them. In this delectable recipe, shrimp will be coated with batter and then deep fried to crunchy perfection.

Makes 6 servings

Ingredients

3 cups of large, deveined and peeled shrimp

Salt and pepper

1 egg, beaten

½ cup yellow cornmeal

½ teaspoon baking powder

½ cup half and half cream

½ cup buttermilk

1 teaspoons salt

¼ teaspoon black pepper

½ teaspoon baking powder

½ teaspoon all-purpose flour

Oil to fry your shrimp

¼ teaspoon pepper

Directions

1. Start by seasoning generously your shrimp with some salt and pepper and then leave them to sit at room temperature for 10 to 15 minutes.

2. Combine the eggs, cornmeal, baking powder, cream, buttermilk, salt, pepper, baking powder and flour together in a mixing bowl and mix until well blended and smooth.

3. Heat the oil in the deep fryer until it reaches 350°F.

4. Dip the shrimp in the batter to coat evenly.

5. Fry the shrimp until they are golden. This will take around 2 minutes.

6. Serve the shrimp hot, with your favorite sauce.

Crab Cakes

Crab cakes make scrumptious appetizers and are popular items on restaurant menus all over, from the East Coast to Kansas. This recipe is super easy and delicious to prepare. You can try these crab cakes to serve to friends on a busy weeknight, or for a spectacular weekend get-together.

Makes 4 servings

Ingredients

½ cup mayonnaise

1 large egg, lightly beaten

1 tablespoon Dijon mustard

1 tablespoon Worcestershire sauce

½ tablespoon hot sauce

1 pound fresh lump crabmeat, drained

1 cup crushed saltines (20 crackers)

1 quart vegetable oil

Tartar sauce (to serve)

Directions

1. Line a baking sheet with waxed paper.
2. In a mixing bowl, stir the mayonnaise, egg, mustard, Worcestershire sauce and hot sauce together.
3. Fold in the crabmeat and the saltines, and allow the mixture to rest for 5 minutes.
4. Shape the mixture into 8 patties, and place them on the baking sheet, cover, and chill for an hour.
5. Heat a few tablespoons of oil in a frying pan, and fry the crab cakes over medium heat for 3 to 4 minutes on each side until golden.
6. Place the fried patties on paper towels to allow the oil to drain.
7. Serve the crab cakes while they are still hot along with tartar sauce, if desired.

Fried Green Tomatoes

You can't have Southern cuisine without fried green tomatoes!

Makes 6 servings

Ingredients

1 large egg

4 tablespoons milk

Vegetable olive oil

1 cup cornmeal

1 cup all-purpose flour

3 large green tomatoes, sliced ¼–inch thick

Ranch dressing for dipping

Directions

1. In a small bowl, combine the egg and milk, and whisk.
2. In a medium sized bowl, mix together the flour and cornmeal.
3. In a heavy and deep skillet, heat oil over medium heat. The oil should cover the bottom of the skillet with about ½ inch in depth.

4. Dredge the tomato slices in the egg mixture followed by the cornmeal mixture, and place the slices in hot oil. Don't overcrowd the skillet. Cook and turn until the tomatoes are golden brown on both sides, about 1-3 minutes per side.

5. Place the fried tomatoes on a plate covered with paper towels to catch the excess oil.

6. Serve warm with your favorite dipping sauce such as a ranch dressing.

Southern Pimento Cheese

This delicious recipe for Pimento cheese can be used for making yummy grilled sandwiches, or as a spread for crackers. Plus, your family will love the spicy kick! We bet the unique combination of creamy, spicy, and salty flavors used in this recipe is good enough to make your friends and family swoon. Don't be surprised if you are bombarded with requests for this treat at every get-together!

Makes 12 Servings

Ingredients

2 cups shredded cheddar cheese

½ cup mayonnaise

¼ teaspoon garlic powder

¼ teaspoon ground cayenne powder

8 ounces cream cheese

1 jalapeno pepper, minced

½ teaspoon onion powder

1 jar diced pimentos, drained

Salt and pepper to taste

Crackers or baguette, to serve

Directions

1. In the bowl of a mixer, place the mayonnaise, garlic powder, onion powder, cheddar cheese, cream cheese, cayenne pepper, pimentos, and jalapeño.
2. Mix all the ingredients at medium speed until thoroughly combined.
3. Season the mixture with salt and pepper, and transfer to a clean bowl.
4. Serve the pimento cheese with crackers or slices of baguette.

Note: pimento cheese is also great in hamburgers!

Deep Fried Dill Pickles

If you are looking for a refreshing snack, look no further than this recipe. These tangy, crispy, and extremely delicious deep fried dill pickles are among the most delicious appetizers out there. Feel free to double the amount of cayenne pepper if you like the pickles to be really spicy.

Makes 12 servings

Ingredients

2 large eggs

1 cup buttermilk

½ teaspoon hot sauce

1 ½ teaspoons black pepper, separated

1 ¼ teaspoons salt, separated

2 ¼ cups all-purpose flour, separated

1 cup corn meal

1 teaspoon cayenne pepper

1 jar dill pickle slices

Vegetable oil for frying

Ranch dressing, or your choice of dip, to serve

Directions

1. In a medium sized bowl, combine the eggs, buttermilk, hot sauce, ¼ cup flour, black pepper, cayenne pepper, and ¼ teaspoon of salt.

2. In another shallow bowl, combine the remaining 2 cups of flour, cornmeal, and the remaining 1 teaspoon of salt and black pepper.

3. Preheat the oil in the deep fryer to 375°F.

4. Remove the pickle slices from the jar and blot them dry with a paper towel.

5. Dip the pickle slices first into the buttermilk mixture and then in the cornmeal mixture.

6. Deep fry the pickles until they appear golden brown, this will take 1 to 2 minutes.

7. Drain the deep fried pickles on a paper towel to get rid of the excess oil.

8. Serve with a dish of ranch dressing for dipping.

Bang Bang Shrimp

Bang Bang shrimp are the best appetizers for hot Southern nights. If you are still craving the famous appetizer from your favorite chain restaurant, this Bang Bang Shrimp recipe is the one to go for. Now you can make delicious shrimp with just the right amount of kick! If you want, use more of the chili sauce to give it a bit more spice.

Makes 4 to 6 Servings

Ingredients

1 pound shrimp, shelled and deveined

½ cup mayonnaise

¼ cup Thai sweet chili sauce

3-5 drops of hot sauce

½ to ¾ cup cornstarch to coat the shrimp

Oil for deep frying

Scallions, chopped, for garnish

Directions

1. In a small bowl, mix the mayonnaise and the sauces together to prepare the coating.
2. Dip the shrimp in the sauce and then gently bread in the cornstarch.

3. Pre-heat the oil in the deep fryer to 350°F.

4. Fry the shrimp until they turn lightly golden, about one minute.

5. Drain the shrimp on a paper towel.

6. Coat the shrimp with the sauces, and serve with chopped scallions to garnish.

Coconut Shrimp

If you are looking for great coconut shrimp, this delectable recipe is just for you. Large juicy shrimp, dipped in batter and then in a mixture of coconut and curry powder, and deep-fried to perfection make great appetizers and snacks. This juicy, delicious dish is incredibly easy to make and your guests will be craving more.

Makes 6-8 servings

Ingredients

1 cup flour

2 pounds large shrimp

½ teaspoon salt

½ teaspoon sugar

1 egg, lightly beaten

2 tablespoons vegetable oil

2/3 cup grated coconut

1 ½ teaspoon curry powder

1 cup ice water

Hot sauce, for serving

Directions

1. Shell and devein the shrimp, leaving the tail intact.
2. In a medium sized bowl, combine the egg, sugar, salt, vegetable oil, ice water, and flour, and beat the mixture until it is smooth.
3. In a separate bowl, mix together the coconut and curry powder.
4. Dip the shrimp into the batter and then into the coconut mixture.
5. Fry the coconut shrimp in hot fat until it turns golden brown on both sides.
6. Serve the shrimp with some hot sauce, if desired.

Shrimp and Grits

Shrimp and grits make a great appetizer; in fact, they take Southern snacks to the next level. They are sometimes called breakfast shrimp but taste great at any time of the day. Now you can use this quick and easy shrimp and grits recipe to wow your family at the dinner or impress guests at weekend events.

Makes 6 servings

Ingredients

1 ½ pounds peeled and deveined shrimp

½ teaspoon hot sauce

3 tablespoons fresh lemon juice

2 bacon slices, chopped

½ cup chopped green onions, plus a few tablespoons for serving

1 ½ cup green bell pepper, chopped

1 cup chicken broth

5 cups water

1 tablespoon butter

1 teaspoon salt

1 ½ cups chopped grits

1 ½ teaspoons minced garlic

¾ cup shredded cheddar cheese

Directions

1. In a medium sized bowl, combine the shrimp, hot sauce, and lemon juice.
2. Cook bacon in a skillet over medium heat until nice and crisp.
3. Add ½ cup green onions, bell pepper and garlic to the pan and allow it to cook for 5 minutes until tender, stirring occasionally.
4. Stir in the broth, shrimp mixture, and ¼ cup of green onions, and allow the mixture to cook for 5 minutes, until the shrimp have completely cooked.
5. In another saucepan, bring the water to a boil and then stir in the grits.
6. Lower the heat to low and allow it to simmer, covered, for 5 minutes until the mixture has thickened.
7. Stir in butter and add salt to taste.
8. Serve the shrimp over the grits, with shredded cheese and green onion sprinkled on top.

Pineapple Cream Cheese Salad

Whipped cream, pineapple, and cream cheese will set the mood for this awesome salad you can prepare within minutes. The festivity of this salad is one of the treats that helps make Christmas so special. Remember, salads cannot get creamier, cooler, or more refreshing than this.

Makes 6-8 servings

Ingredients

½ cup mayonnaise

1 cup whipped cream

1 package lemon gelatin

1 can crushed pineapple

1 cup cream cheese

1 cup water

⅓ cup chopped walnuts

Directions

1. In a medium sized bowl combine the whipped cream and mayonnaise together and then place in the refrigerator. Allow the mixture to cool for an hour.
2. Combine the pineapple and water in a saucepan and bring to a boil. Reduce heat to low.

3. Add the lemon gelatin to the mixture, stir continuously until dissolved completely, and then allow it to cool.
4. Before the gelatin sets, add the whipped cream mixture together with the cream cheese. Stir to combine well. Place in the refrigerator for 1-2 hours, or until set.
5. Sprinkle the walnuts on top. Serve chilled.

Main Entrées

Meat Pie

The Southern styled meat pie is among the most favorite comfort foods for pie lovers everywhere. This recipe is packed with flavor and makes a delicious meal. Reach for this great dish if you are looking for an easy, convenient dinner idea.

Makes 8-10 servings

Ingredients

1 pound ground pork

1 pound ground beef

2 celery stalks, finely diced

1 green bell pepper, chopped

1 large baking potato, peeled and finely chopped

1 bay leaf

1 teaspoon dried thyme leaves

3 cloves of garlic, minced

1 small carrot

1 large onion

1 cup hot water

1 teaspoon Worcestershire sauce

2 beef bouillon cubes

2 tablespoons chopped fresh parsley

Salt free seasoning blend to taste

Salt and pepper to taste

1 egg, separated

2 tablespoons of water

2 sheets frozen puff pastry

2 cups shredded cheddar cheese

Cooking spray

Directions

1. Preheat the oven to 350°F, and coat a 9x13 inch dish with cooking spray.
2. Put a large nonstick skillet over medium high heat and mix the ground pork and beef, cooking until brown and crumbly, about 6-8 minutes. Discard the excess grease.
3. Add the bell pepper, celery, onions and stir, then cover the pan and reduce the heat to medium.
4. Stir frequently, until the vegetables have softened and the onions are translucent, about 4-6 minutes.
5. Make a well in the center of the skillet; place the garlic on the bottom of the pan for a few seconds, and then blend with the meat.
6. Add the parsley, carrot, bay leaf, thyme, potato, Worcestershire sauce, seasoning blend, and salt and pepper to taste.

7. In a bowl, dissolve the bouillon cubes in hot water then pour it into the meat mixture and mix it well. Bring to a boil then reduce the heat from medium to low. Cover and simmer for 10 to 15 minutes until the carrots have softened.

8. In the prepared baking dish, lay one sheet of puff pastry. Gently push the pastry into the corners of the baking dish. Gently spoon the meat mixture into the crust and spread evenly. Avoid adding liquid to the pie as it will cause it to become soggy. Top the mixture with cheddar cheese.

9. In a small bowl, whisk together the egg yolk and a tablespoon of water.

10. Brush the edges of the bottom of the puff pastry sheet.

11. Lay the second sheet of puff pastry on the top and seal the edges by pressing with a fork.

12. Mix the egg white with remaining tablespoon of water, and brush the top surface of the pastry. Poke holes with a fork to vent the crust.

13. Preheat the oven to 350°F and bake the pie until the pastry has turned golden brown. Keep checking your pie after every 15 minutes to prevent your pie from over burning. Serve hot.

Kentucky Hot Browns

In seek of comfort? This famous Southern recipe is sure to become your favorite, topped with roasted turkey and delicious Parmesan cheese. You will find yourself in food heaven!

Makes 4 servings

Ingredients

4 thick white bread slices

12 ounces sliced roasted turkey

2 tomatoes, sliced

8 bacon slices, cooked

1 cup shredded Parmesan cheese

Mornay Sauce (recipe follows)

Directions

1. Preheat broiler and place oven rack on the upper position at about 6 inches from heat source.
2. On a baking dish, place bread slices and broil until golden brown on each side, about 1 minute per side.
3. Arrange bread slices on 4 lightly greased individual baking dishes, and top with turkey slices.

4. Pour warm Mornay sauce over the turkey, and sprinkle each evenly with the Parmesan cheese.

5. Place under the broiler until the cheese is melted and golden, about 2-4 minutes.

6. Top with tomato slices and bacon, and serve.

Mornay Sauce

Yields approx. 1 ½ cups

Ingredients

½ cup butter

⅓ cup all-purpose flour

1 ½ cups milk

¼ teaspoon salt

¼ teaspoon pepper

½ cup shredded Parmesan

Directions

1. Melt butter in a saucepan over medium- high heat.
2. Whisk in flour, and cook for 1 minute, whisking constantly.
3. Add milk and bring it to a boil. Reduce heat to medium-low, and continue cooking until it has thickened, about 3-4 minutes.
4. Whisk in Parmesan cheese, salt and pepper. Continue stirring until the cheese is melted. Serve immediately.

Jambalaya

If you are craving a New Orleans classic, this recipe for Jambalaya is the perfect option for you. This spicy rice is all you need to fill yourself to the brim. Treat your taste buds to deep flavors with this authentic Jambalaya recipe any time you want. After all, you just cannot resist the aroma of sautéed aromatic onion, celery, and peppers, with herbs, garlic, and spices.

Makes 4 servings

Ingredients

1 pound chicken breast, diced
1 medium sized yellow onion, chopped
2 tablespoons butter
½ pound andouille sausage, sliced in ¼ inch slices
1 green bell pepper, diced
1 stalk celery, diced
3 cloves of garlic, minced
2 teaspoons hot sauce
2 cups chicken broth
1 teaspoon Worcestershire sauce
1 can diced tomatoes
2 bay leaves
¾ teaspoon salt
½ teaspoon black pepper each
½ pound raw shrimp, deveined
2 tablespoons Creole seasoning
1 cup long grain rice
4 green onions, thinly sliced, for garnish

Directions

1. Combine all the spices for the Creole seasoning and place in a clean coffee grinder. Grind until you have a fine powder, and store the powder in an airtight jar.
2. Place the chicken in a large bowl and sprinkle with 1 tablespoon of the Creole seasoning. Set it aside to rest.
3. Place a large skillet on medium high heat and melt the butter.
4. Cook the chicken and the sausage until browned, and drain excess fat.
5. Add the bell pepper, garlic, onion, and celery, and cook for 4 minutes.
6. Add the rice, and the remaining tablespoon of Creole seasoning, diced tomatoes, hot sauce, salt, black pepper, and Worcestershire sauce, and stir the mixture until it is thoroughly combined.
7. Add the chicken broth and bay leaves, and bring the mixture to a boil. Reduce the heat to medium low, cover the pot, and allow it to simmer for 15 minutes. Give it a stir around the halfway point.
8. Finally, add the shrimp, cover, and then allow the Jambalaya to simmer for another 10 minutes until the rice turns tender and thoroughly cooked.
9. Place in a serving dish and enjoy with a sprinkle of green onions, while it is still hot!

Grandma's Fried Chicken

Nothing can compete with Southern Fried Chicken, and this recipe is great for feeding a crowd. Simply kick back, enjoy, and relax as you devour this delicious meal. Those of you who want to add a satisfying twist to this classic can pour in a little extra hot sauce.

Makes 4 to 6 servings

Ingredients

1 chicken (2-3 pounds), cut into 8 pieces
Peanut oil for frying (enough to cover the chicken in the saucepan)
Dipping sauce for serving

Marinade
4 cups buttermilk
1 teaspoon (or more) hot sauce
1 teaspoon salt
1 teaspoon black pepper

Dredging Mixture
1 teaspoon garlic powder
1 teaspoon cayenne pepper (or more if you like spicier)
1 teaspoon salt
1 teaspoon black pepper
1 teaspoon cumin
1 teaspoon dry thyme
1 teaspoon baking powder
2½ cups all-purpose flour

Directions

1. In a large mixing bowl, add the buttermilk, hot sauce, salt and black pepper. Whisk to combine well. Add the chicken pieces. The buttermilk mixture should cover the chicken. Using your hands, make sure the chicken pieces are well covered in buttermilk. Refrigerate for at least 3 hours and up to 12 hours. Remove the chicken from the refrigerator at least 1 hour before cooking to bring it to room temperature.

2. In a large, deep pot, heat the peanut oil to 350°F. You can also use a deep cast iron skillet, filled to the ¾ with the oil.

3. Prepare the dredging mixture in a shallow bowl by adding all the ingredients and mixing well.

4. Remove the chicken pieces from the buttermilk mixture and dredge into the flour one piece at a time. Shake gently to remove excess flout. Carefully lower it into the hot oil with a slotted spoon.

5. Do not crowd all the chicken pieces together; cook half the chicken at a time until crispy and brown, about 15 minutes. Turn the chicken over after 7 or 8 minutes. Once cooked, remove the chicken pieces with a slotted spoon and drain on a paper towels.

6. To check the doneness of the chicken, poke the chicken with a fork on the thickest part of the chicken to make sure the juices run clear or that the internal temperature should reads at least 165°F on an instant reading meat thermometer when inserted in the thickest part of the chicken piece without touching a bone.

7. Enjoy while hot, with the dipping sauce of your choice!

Barbecue Pulled Pork Sandwiches

These easy (only three ingredients!) and delicious barbecue pulled pork sandwiches make a heavenly meal that will satisfy your Southern cravings. Pork slow-cooked in spices and sauce is great for lunch or dinner on any day. In fact, you can put it on before going out to work – this juicy pork will be ready when you get home.

Makes 12 servings

Ingredients

1 can beef broth

1 bottle barbecue sauce

3 pounds boneless pork ribs

12 Buns

Favorite toppings such as tomatoes and coleslaw

French fries, for serving

Directions

1. Pour the beef broth into a slow cooker and add the pork ribs. Cook on high heat for 4 hours, until the meat is tender and shreds easily.
2. Preheat the oven to 350°F.

3. Place the shredded pork in a cast iron skillet or Dutch oven and stir in the barbecue sauce.

4. Bake the pork in the oven for 30 minutes until it is properly heated through.

5. Place a generous amount of the pull pork on a bun, top with toppings. Serve with French fries if desired.

Oyster Stew

This recipe for creamy oyster stew has been passed down from generation to generation of New Orleans families. If you wish to give a simple, refreshing twist to delicious seafood flavor, this oyster stew recipe is the one to go for.

Makes 4 to 6 servings

Ingredients

1 pint shucked fresh oysters

¼ cup butter

1 shallot, minced

1 clove of garlic, minced

2 tablespoons all-purpose flour

2 cups warm whole or 2% milk

1 cup warm half-and-half cream

1 tablespoon hot sauce

2 tablespoons sherry

1/8 teaspoon celery salt

½ teaspoon Worcestershire sauce

Kosher salt and freshly crack black pepper

Fresh lemon juice

Oyster crackers

Directions

1. Drain the oysters, reserving the oyster liquor.

2. In a small saucepan, heat the oyster liquor and half-and-half over medium heat, stirring continuously for 3 to 4 minutes, until the mixture starts to steam.

3. Add the oysters, cooking for 4 to 5 minutes until the edges of the oysters start to curl.

4. Remove from the heat. With a slotted spoon, transfer the oysters to a plate and reserve.

5. In a large sauce pan, melt the butter, and add garlic and shallot. Cook, stirring occasionally, for 4 minutes until tender.

6. Sprinkle the flour over the mixture and cook, whisking continuously, for 1 to 2 minutes.

7. Slowly add milk, cream, hot sauce, sherry, celery salt, and Worcestershire sauce. Stir until it begins to thicken, then add the oysters.

8. Cook on medium to low heat, stirring occasionally, until it has warmed through.

9. Season the stew with salt and pepper to taste, and serve with a splash of lemon juice and crackers.

Southern Fried Pork Chops

Looking for a tender, juicy pork chop recipe that turns out perfectly every time? Well, you need look no further. Southern fried pork chops are simple to make, yet so delicious. You can serve them for lunch, dinner, or even as a late brunch.

Makes 4 servings

Ingredients

4 thin cut, bone-in pork chops

1 cup buttermilk

Vegetable oil for frying

1 cup self-rising flour

Seasoned salt and pepper to taste

Directions

1. Season each side of the pork with seasoned salt and pepper.
2. Pour the buttermilk into a shallow bowl, and cover a plate or pie pan with flour.
3. Dip the pork chops first onto the buttermilk and then coat with the flour evenly on both sides.

4. Refrigerate for 30 minutes.

5. Heat a few tablespoons of oil in a large pan over high heat, enough to cook four chops at a time.

6. Fry the pork chops, making sure each side is browned, about 8 minutes per side.

Louisiana Red Bean and Rice

This authentic recipe is a favorite from Louisiana. No matter when you make it, it will be impossible for you to keep your hands off it. Add a splash of cider vinegar and you will be amazed by the delicious flavor. Ask any person who grew up in Louisiana, they'll tell you how this simple recipe has changed the dimensions of Southern cuisine.

Makes 8 servings

Ingredients

1 pound andouille sausage, sliced

1 pound kidney beans

¼ cup olive oil

1 large onion, chopped

1 green bell pepper, chopped

2 celery stalks, chopped

2 tablespoons garlic, minced

½ teaspoon cayenne pepper

1 tablespoon dried parsley

¼ teaspoon dried sage

1 teaspoon dried thyme

1 teaspoon Cajun seasoning

2 cups long grain white rice

4 cups beef broth

6 cups water

2 bay leaves

Directions

1. Soak the beans in water in a large saucepan overnight.

2. In a medium sized skillet, heat the oil over medium heat, and sauté onion, celery, bell pepper, and garlic in olive oil for 3 to 4 minutes

3. Rinse the beans and cover them with 6 cups of water.

4. Add cooked vegetables to the beans, and stir in the cayenne pepper, parsley, sage, thyme, bay leaves, and Cajun seasoning.

5. Bring the mixture to a boil, and reduce the heat to medium low, and simmer for 2 ½ hours.

6. Stir the sausage into the beans and allow it to simmer for 30 minutes.

7. In a saucepan, boil 4 cups beef broth, and add the rice. Reduce the heat, cover it and allow it to simmer for 20 minutes. You can also use a rice cooker.

8. Serve the bean mixture over the hot rice.

Double Crust Chicken Pot Pie

Want to discover a classic Southern secret? Well, this recipe is the one you need to check out. The Double Crust Chicken pot pie is enough to dazzle your guests and bring the Southern atmosphere home. The golden crust will win you rave reviews at the dinner table.

Makes 6 to 8 servings

Ingredients

1 large egg

1 can chicken broth

½ cup butter

½ cup all-purpose flour

2 medium leeks, sliced

1 cup carrots, cut in matchsticks

3 cups of cooked chicken, chopped

½ teaspoon salt

½ teaspoon ground pepper

1 ½ cups frozen cubed hash browns with onions and peppers

⅓ cup chopped parsley

1 package of puff pastry

Directions

1. Preheat the oven to 375°F.

2. In a large skillet, heat the butter over medium heat, add the leeks and sauté for 3 minutes.

3. Sprinkle flour over the mixture, and continue to stir constantly for 3 minutes.

4. Whisking constantly, blend in the chicken broth and bring the mixture to a boil.

5. Remove from the heat, and add the chicken, carrots, parsley, salt, pepper, hash browns, and stir to combine.

6. Coat a clean surface with flour, and roll each pastry sheet into a 12x10 inch rectangle.

7. Fit the sheet into a 9 inch pie plate, making sure the narrow sides cover the rim of the pie plate. Scoop in the chicken mixture into the pastry.

8. Place the remaining pastry sheet over the chicken mixture in the opposite direction of the bottom sheet

9. Tuck and press the edges around the dish, and press the edges with a fork to seal the crust. Trim the excess.

10. In a separate bowl, whisk a large egg with 1 tablespoon of water, and brush the mixture over the top of the pie.

11. Bake the pie in the oven at 375°F on the middle rack of the oven for 55 to 60 minutes until the crust starts to brown.

12. Let the pie rest for about 15 minutes before serving.

Chunky Beef Chili

This hearty bowl of chunky chili is just what you need to remind you of the traditional American South chili seasonings.

Makes 9 Cups

Ingredients

4 pounds boneless chuck roast, cubed

2 6 oz. cans of tomato paste

2 15 oz. cans tomato sauce

2 tablespoons chili powder

2 teaspoons granulated garlic

1 teaspoon ground cumin

1 teaspoon ground oregano

1 teaspoon salt

½ teaspoon onion powder

½ teaspoon ground black pepper

¼ teaspoon ground red pepper

1 teaspoon paprika

For Topping

Chopped onions

Crushed tortilla chips

Shredded cheese

Sour cream

Directions

1. Brown the meat in batches in a Dutch oven over medium high heat.

2. Remove the meat from the pot, but keep the drippings in the pot. Add chili powder and cook for 2 minutes, stirring constantly.

3. Place the beef back in the pot, and add the tomato paste with the tomato sauce, oregano, cumin, paprika, black pepper, red pepper, salt, onion powder, and granulated garlic. Stir well.

4. Bring the mixture to a boil, reduce the heat to low and allow it to simmer, uncovered for 1 ½ hours, stirring occasionally. Serve hot, garnished with toppings.

Crawfish Pie

This delicious Southern style pie is loaded with the goodness of vegetables that even the pickiest eaters will enjoy. A little hint of heat from cayenne pepper can give your taste buds an exciting treat. There's no special day to try this recipe — any time is good!

Makes 6 Servings

Ingredients

¼ cup butter

½ cup celery, chopped

1 cup onion, chopped

½ cup green pepper, chopped

1 ½ teaspoons salt

1 prepared deep dish pie crust, 9 inch

1 cup diced tomatoes

½ teaspoon ground cayenne pepper

2 tablespoons all-purpose flour

1/8 teaspoon white pepper

12 ounces peeled crawfish tails

1 cup water

Directions

1. Line the deep dish pie plate with the pie crust, and set aside.

2. In a large skillet, melt the butter over medium heat, and stir in the celery, onion, green pepper, salt, cayenne pepper, and white pepper, and cook until the vegetables are tender, about 5 minutes.

3. Stir in the tomatoes and the crawfish, reduce the heat, and allow the mixture to cook for 3 minutes to blend the flavors. Stir occasionally.

4. In a large bowl, whisk the flour and water together until smooth, pour the mixture into the skillet.

5. Stir the filling and bring it to a simmer, stirring until the mixture thickens.

6. Remove the mixture from the heat and allow it to rest 20 to 30 minutes

7. Preheat the oven to 400°F.

8. Pour the filling into the prepared pie crust, and bake it in the oven until the crust turns golden brown and the filling starts to bubble, 30 to 40 minutes.

9. Take the pie out of the oven and allow it to cool for 10 minutes before serving.

Chicken and Dumplings

This is a favorite classic in the South. Filled with aromatic flavors of thyme, garlic, and heavenly seasonings, this dish will soon become a favorite in your household too. You can whip up this old fashioned Southern recipe any time you're craving some soul satisfying soup.

Makes 11 Servings

Ingredients

1 whole chicken

½ teaspoon dried thyme

½ teaspoon garlic powder

1 teaspoon chicken bouillon granules

1 cup milk

1 teaspoon bacon drippings

3 cups self-rising flour

1½ teaspoons of salt, separated

¾ teaspoon pepper

½ tablespoon poultry seasoning

⅓ cup shortening

Water

Directions

1. Place the chicken in a Dutch oven, and sprinkle with, garlic powder, thyme, ½ teaspoon of salt, ½ teaspoon of pepper. Fill halfway with water and bring it to a boil.

2. Cover with the lid, and reduce the heat to medium low, allow it to simmer for at least an hour.

3. Remove the chicken to a platter, but reserve the broth.

4. Allow the chicken to cool for 30 minutes, then remove the skin and bone and shred the meat into small pieces.

5. Skim the fat from the broth. Put the shredded chicken back into the pot, and add 1 teaspoon of salt, ¼ teaspoon of pepper, and bouillon granules. Simmer the mixture while preparing the dumplings.

6. In a bowl, combine the flour and poultry seasoning. Cut the shortening and bacon drippings with a pastry blender until crumbly. Stir in the milk until the dough forms a ball. Do not overmix.

7. Turn the dough out onto a lightly floured surface. Roll to ⅛ inch thickness, and cut it into 1 inch pieces.

8. Slowly, drop the dumplings in to the simmering broth, stirring it gently. Cover and simmer for 25 minutes.

9. Serve in a large serving dish.

Gumbo

This heavenly recipe from New Orleans will have you going for second servings and maybe even more. Gumbo is one of the shiniest gems in the crown of Southern cuisine. Simply let all the flavors blend into the meat before you let the good times roll.

Makes 8 to 10 servings

Ingredients

¼ cup vegetable oil

3 large boneless skinless chicken breasts

1 pound smoked sausage

1 large onion, chopped

5 tablespoons butter

3 stalks celery, chopped

1 green bell pepper, seeded and chopped

½ cup all-purpose flour

¼ cup Worcestershire sauce

5 beef bouillon cubes

4 cups hot water

8 cloves of garlic, minced

4 green onions

½ pound shrimp, peeled, cooked and deveined

1 can stewed tomatoes (14 ounces)

¼ bunch flat leaf parsley, plus some more for garnish

2 cups sliced okra

Salt and pepper to taste

Directions

1. Season the chicken with salt and pepper.
2. Heat the oil in a heavy bottomed Dutch oven over medium high heat.
3. Cook the chicken until browned on both sides, remove, and set aside.
4. Cook the sausage, stirring until browned, remove, and set aside.
5. Sprinkle flour over the drippings, and add two tablespoons of butter, allowing it to cook over medium heat. Whisk constantly until it begins to brown; this will take about 8-10 minutes.
6. Return the Dutch oven back to low heat, add the remaining 3 tablespoons of butter.
7. Add the garlic, onion, green pepper, okra, and celery and allow it to cook for 10 minutes, stirring often.
8. Next, mix in Worcestershire sauce, ¼ bunch of parsley, salt, and pepper to taste.
9. Dissolve the bouillon cubes in 4 cups of hot water and add it to the pot, together with the chicken and sausage, bring the mixture to a boil. Reduce the heat, allow it to simmer for 45 minutes to an hour.
10. Garnish with parsley, green onions and shrimp. Serve hot!

Fried Catfish

Fried catfish is an epic Southern tradition. This delicious recipe is sure to satisfy. Seasoned, and then fried to perfection, this fish will have you hooked.

Makes 6 servings

Ingredients

6 catfish fillets

1 quart peanut oil

1 cup all-purpose flour

1 cup stone ground cornmeal

1 teaspoon seafood seasoning

¼ teaspoon ground pepper

¼ teaspoon hot paprika

½ teaspoon kosher salt

¾ cup low fat butter milk

Sliced lemon, for serving

Directions

1. Heat the peanut oil in a Dutch oven on the stovetop to 350°F.
2. In a shallow dish, whisk together the cornmeal and flour.

3. In a separate bowl, combine the kosher salt, paprika, seafood seasoning, and pepper.
4. Pour the buttermilk into a third shallow dish.
5. Season the catfish on both sides with the spice mixture, and then dip the catfish in the buttermilk, holding it over the pan so that the excess drips off.
6. Dip the catfish in the cornmeal mixture, coating it evenly on both sides.
7. Let the fillets rest on a cooling rack for 5 minutes.
8. Gently lower the fillets, 2 at a time, into the hot oil, and fry until they are golden brown, about 5 to 6 minutes.
9. Gently place the fillets on a cooking rack to drain.
10. Repeat until all the fillets are fried, and serve hot with lemon slices.

King Ranch Chicken Casserole

This classic Southern King Ranch Casserole recipe is bursting with the goodness of cheese, peppers, and chicken. It's also a super easy fix to dinner time confusion. More importantly, this recipe is always a hit with the crowd – we bet everyone will love it!

Makes 8 servings

Ingredients

2 cups cooked chicken, chopped

2 tablespoons vegetable oil

1 large onion, chopped

1 large green bell pepper, chopped

¼ teaspoon black pepper

¼ teaspoon salt

¼ teaspoon garlic powder

1 can cream of mushroom soup (10 ¾ ounce)

1 can diced tomatoes with green chilies (10 ounce)

12 corn tortillas (6 inch)

2 cups cheddar cheese, shredded

Directions

1. Heat the oil in a large skillet over medium high heat, and sauté the onions and bell pepper until tender.

2. Stir in the chicken, salt, black pepper, garlic powder, mushroom soup, and tomatoes, and remove from the heat.

3. Lightly grease a 13x9 inch baking dish. Tear in the tortillas into 1 inch pieces and layer ⅓ of the tortillas in the bottom of the baking dish.

4. Top the layer of tortillas with ⅓ of the chicken mixture, then with 2/3 cup cheese. Repeat layers twice.

5. Bake the dish in the oven at 350°F for 30 to 35 minutes.

6. Let the casserole rest for 10 minutes before serving.

Pot Roast

A nice bowl of pot roast is a hit anywhere. Look no further than this superb, extremely tasty and classic southern pot roast recipe if you have been searching for something to serve at weekend parties or family dinners. This dish is best served with mashed potatoes and roasted green beans.

Makes 6 to 8 servings

Ingredients

1 boneless bottom round roast (3 to 4 pounds)

¼ cup vegetable oil

2 yellow onions, peeled and quartered

3 cloves garlic, crushed

2 cups beef broth

2 bay leaves

2 fresh thyme sprigs

3 carrots, sliced into ½ inch pieces

1 cup red wine

1 tablespoon tomato paste

Kosher salt and black pepper to taste

Fresh parsley leaves, chopped

Directions

1. Preheat oven to 350°F.

2. Season the roast with both sides with salt and pepper.

3. Heat oil in a Dutch oven over medium high heat and sear the roast on both sides. Remove the roast from the pot and set aside.

4. Combine the tomato paste, garlic, onions in the pot, and allow the mixture to cook until it has colored.

5. Add the thyme, bay leaves, broth, and wine, and place the roast in the liquid.

6. Bring the mixture to a simmer, then cover and place in the oven.

7. Allow the pot to roast for 1 ½ hours, and then add the carrots. Cook for another hour.

8. Transfer the roast to a cutting board and allow it to rest for 10 to 20 minutes before carving.

9. Skim the fat from the braising liquid, and serve it piping hot over the meat, with freshly chopped parsley.

Southern Chicken Fried Steak

The Southern Chicken Fried Steak is a traditional staple in most Southern homes. It is easy to make and tastes great too. Even the pickiest eaters love it!

Makes 6 servings

Ingredients

2 cups all-purpose flour

2 eggs

2 pounds boneless chicken breast cutlets

¼ cup oil for frying

Herbs to taste

Salt and pepper to taste

Hot sauce for serving

Directions

1. In a large bowl, combine the herb seasonings, salt, pepper, and flour.
2. In another bowl, beat the eggs.
3. Coat each veal cutlet first in the flour mixture, then dip into egg, followed by another coat in the flour mixture.
4. In a skillet, heat oil over medium high heat. Place veal cutlets into hot oil and fry until each side is browned, about 5 minutes per side.
5. Serve with a side of hot sauce.

Sides

Red Potato Salad

This pretty potato salad has a great aroma and flavor, plus it goes well with any menu. Aside from the combination of rich potatoes and mayonnaise, this wholesome potato salad is filling and satisfying. For a twist on the flavors, feel free to add your favorite herbs and spices.

Ingredients

6-7 medium sized red potatoes, scrubbed and cut into pieces

1 cup mayonnaise

½ tablespoon brown mustard

¾ teaspoon white vinegar

¾ teaspoon celery salt

4 hardboiled eggs, roughly chopped

1 to 2 celery stalks, thinly sliced

¾ cup onions, sliced

4 slices of bacon, cooked and crumbled

Salt and pepper to taste

Freshly chopped chives for garnishing

Directions

1. Put the potato chunks in a medium sized sauce pan and then cover with cold water. Bring to a boil over medium high heat.

2. After the potatoes have boiled, reduce the heat to medium low and continue to cook for 8 to 10 minutes until they are tender.

3. Drain the potatoes and then set it aside.

4. In a separate large bowl, combine the mayonnaise, mustard, vinegar, celery salt, eggs, onions, bacon and celery. Mix all the ingredients well and then finally add the potatoes.

5. Season to taste with salt and pepper.

6. Chill the salad over night or for at least 2 hours, and garnish with chives before serving.

Buttermilk Cast Iron Cornbread

Celebrate Southern cuisine with this heavenly recipe for Southern cornbread. You can serve this quintessential southern staple with soups, stews, and salads to wow your guests and family.

Makes 6 servings

Ingredients

2 cups buttermilk

1 cup cornmeal

1 teaspoon baking powder

½ teaspoon baking soda

1 cup flour, all purpose

2 tablespoons white sugar

2 eggs

3 tablespoons butter

Directions

1. Preheat the oven to 375°F.
2. Add the butter to a 10" cast iron skillet.
3. Place in the oven while you make the batter.
4. In a large bowl, whisk together the flour, baking soda, and baking powder.
5. Add the cornmeal, and mix until the ingredients are well blended.

6. In a separate bowl, whisk together the eggs and buttermilk.

7. Add the sugar, and blend until the sugar is dissolved.

8. Remove the cast iron skillet from the oven, and tilt the skillet until it is completely coated in butter.

9. Pour the remaining butter into the egg mixture.

10. Add the wet ingredients into the dry, and mix until the batter is smooth.

11. Pour the batter into the cast iron skillet, and place in the oven.

12. Bake for 25 to 30 minutes or until the cornbread golden brown and springs back when pressed.

13. Serve warm.

Classic Southern Creamy Coleslaw

Crispy, tangy, and crunchy, there is so much to love about this recipe. In fact, this crunchy version of coleslaw looks bright and tastes exactly how it should.

Makes 8 Servings

Ingredients

1 head cabbage, finely shredded
2 carrots, finely chopped
2 tablespoons finely chopped onion
⅓ cup white sugar
¼ cup buttermilk
2 tablespoons lemon juice
2 tablespoons distilled white vinegar
½ teaspoon salt
1/8 teaspoon ground black pepper

Directions

1. In a large salad bowl, mix together carrots, onions, and cabbage.
2. In a separate bowl, whisk sugar, buttermilk, lemon juice, vinegar, and salt and pepper until the mixture is smooth and the sugar has dissolved.
3. Pour the dressing onto the cabbage mixture.
4. Cover the bowl and refrigerate for at least 2 hours.
5. Mix coleslaw again before serving.

Feta Stuffed Tomatoes

This is a heavenly side dish bursting with the flavors of fresh herbs and delicious vegetables. The stuffing is healthy and scrumptious.

Makes 8 servings

Ingredients

4 large tomatoes
¼ cup fine, dry bread crumbs
1 tablespoons olive oil
4 ounces crumbled feta cheese
2 tablespoons green onions, sliced
2 tablespoons chopped fresh parsley
Parsley to garnish

Directions

1. Preheat the oven to 350°F.
2. Slice tomatoes in half horizontally, scooping out the pulp, and keeping the outside intact.
3. Discard the tomato seeds and roughly chop up the pulp.
4. Combine the feta cheese, pulp, green onions, parsley, and olive oil in a medium sized bowl.
5. Spoon in the mixture evenly into the tomato shells.
6. Place the tomato shells in a 9x9 inch baking dish.
7. Bake the tomatoes for 15 minutes.
8. Garnish with parsley, and serve.

Cream Cheese Mashed Potatoes

This creamy recipe for mashed potatoes is all you need to brighten up your weekend meals. You can also prepare this side dish ahead of time and reheat when needed.

Makes 10 servings

Ingredients

2 packages of cream cheese (3 ounces each)

5 pounds baking potatoes

1 container of sour cream (8 ounces)

2 teaspoons onion salt

½ cup butter or margarine

½ cup milk

Parsley, to garnish

Cooking spray

Directions

1. Preheat the oven to 325°F.
2. Peel potatoes and cut them into 1 inch cubes.
3. Bring a large pot of water to a boil, and cook the potatoes for 15 to 20 minutes until tender.
4. Drain the potatoes and place them in a large mixing bowl.

5. Add the cream cheese, sour cream, margarine, milk, and onion salt, and beat all the ingredients at medium speed with electric mixer until smooth and fluffy.

6. Greased a 3-quart baking dish with cooking spray. Spoon in the potatoes mixture, and bake for 10 minutes until heated through.

7. Garnish with parsley and serve.

Fried Okra

Fried okra is a favorite Southern classic! Drenched with batter and fried to perfection, this is something you do not want to miss out on. This perfectly crispy okra will have you and your guests coming back for more.

Makes 4 servings

Ingredients

10 pods of okra

1 cup cornmeal

¼ teaspoon ground pepper

½ cup vegetable oil

¼ teaspoon salt

1 egg

Kosher salt and white pepper vinegar, for serving

Directions

1. Beat the egg in a large bowl, and soak the okra in it for 10 minutes.
2. In another, medium sized bowl, combine salt, pepper, and cornmeal.
3. Heat oil in a large skillet over medium high heat.

4. Dip the okra in the cornmeal mixture, coating it evenly on all sides.
5. Place okra in the hot oil, reduce the heat to medium low as the okra starts to turn brown. Stir continuously.
6. Drain on paper towels, and serve with salt and pepper vinegar.

Southern Style Collard Greens

You've read about collard greens, but have you tried them? Because this recipe yields the tastiest greens, you need look no further if you have a special affection for them. And don't forget to make this recipe an integral part of your traditional Southern feast if you love soulful flavors.

Makes 10 servings

Ingredients

2 smoked ham hocks

2 sweet onions, finely chopped

3 containers of chicken broth (32 ounces each)

4 cloves of garlic, finely chopped

3 packages of collard greens (1 pound each)

2 tablespoons white vinegar

1 ½ teaspoons salt

¾ teaspoon black pepper

2 tablespoons white sugar

⅓ cup vinegar

Directions

1. Combine the garlic, onions, and ham hocks in a stock pot. Add the chicken broth and cook the mixture over medium to low heat until the meat is tender and starts to fall off the bone, about 2 hours.

2. Stir the collard greens, salt, black pepper, sugar, and vinegar into the broth mixture, and cook until the greens have reached the desired texture and tenderness, about 2 hours. Serve hot.

Pickled Green Tomatoes

These crunchy and delicious pickled green tomatoes will go perfectly with ham or grilled chicken. Try this recipe as a perfect relish for any lunch or dinner plate.

Makes 6 pints

Ingredients

5 pounds green tomatoes, chopped

2 tablespoons pickling salt

1 large onion, chopped

2 cups cider vinegar

1 ½ cups firmly packed brown sugar

2 teaspoons celery seed

2 teaspoons whole allspice

2 teaspoons mustard seeds

½ teaspoon whole cloves

3 cups water

Directions

1. Season the tomatoes and onions with pickling salt, and let it stand for 4 to 7 hours.
2. Drain the ingredients and pat dry with paper towels, set aside.

3. In a Dutch oven, combine vinegar and brown sugar, and cook over medium heat. Stir the constantly until the brown sugar dissolves.

4. Place the celery seed, allspice, mustard seeds, and whole cloves in a 6 inch square of cheese cloth, and tie it with a string.

5. Add the spice bag, along with the tomatoes, onions, and 3 cups of water to the vinegar mixture.

6. Bring the ingredients to a boil, stirring constantly. Reduce the heat and allow the mixture to simmer, stirring occasionally, for 25 minutes, until the onions and tomatoes are tender.

7. Remove and discard the spice bag.

8. Pour the hot pickles into mason jars, tap the jars to remove any air bubbles and cover the jar with the metal lid.

9. Process in boiling water bath for at least 10 minutes.

Summer Squash Casserole

Summer squash casserole is one of the most innovative Southern side dishes of all time. It goes great with turkey or grilled chicken. You will find this side dish an ideal pick for nearly every special occasion, holiday, or get together.

Makes 8 to 10 servings

Ingredients

2 pounds yellow summer squash

1 large onion, chopped

7 tablespoons butter, divided

1 large clove garlic, chopped

½ green bell pepper, chopped

½ red bell pepper, chopped

4 slices plain white bread, toasted

1 jalapeño pepper, seeded and chopped

24 round buttery crackers, crumbled in a food processor

½ cup heavy whipping cream

½ pound sharp cheddar cheese

1 teaspoon salt

1 teaspoon sugar

4 large eggs, beaten

¼ teaspoon cayenne pepper

Directions

1. Heat the oven to 350°F, and grease a 2-quart baking dish with butter.
2. Cut the squash to ½ inch thick slices, and boil in salted water for 10 minutes, until cooked through.
3. Drain the squash, and purée in a food processor.
4. Over medium heat, melt 6 tablespoon of butter, add onion, peppers and garlic, and cook until the mixture is tender.
5. In the meantime, put the toast in a food processor, melt the remaining butter and combine it with the crumbs.
6. Combine the squash puree, garlic, crackers, cheese, peppers, and onion together, and mix well. Stir in the sugar, cream, egg and seasonings, and blend.
7. Pour the mixture in a baking dish.
8. Top it with toast crumbs, and bake for 40 minutes until browned.

Fresh Corn Cakes

Are you craving something like pancakes? Dive into this appetizing side dish, made with fresh corn, mozzarella cheese, and chives.

Makes 3 dozen

Ingredients

3 large eggs

¾ cup milk

1 cup fresh corn kernels

¾ cup all-purpose flour

3 tablespoons melted butter

¾ cup yellow or white cornmeal

2 tablespoons chopped fresh chives

1 8-ounces package fresh mozzarella cheese, grated

1 teaspoon salt

1 teaspoon ground pepper

Chives for serving

Directions

1. Pulse the corn, eggs, milk, and butter in a food processor 3 to 4 times until the corn is coarsely chopped.

2. Combine the flour, cornmeal, cheese, chives, and salt and pepper together in a large bowl. Stir in the corn mixture until the dry ingredients are moistened.

3. Spoon 1/8 cup batter for each cake onto a greased non-stick pan.

4. Cook the cakes for 2 to 3 minutes per side until browned.

5. Garnish with chopped chives and serve.

Okra and Pecan Casserole

The flavor of pecans, combined with okra and crisp breading is a southern side dish you cannot get enough of. If your goal is to bring the delicious combination of pecan and breading into one recipe and stay low on the carb count, this dish is the one you should go for.

Makes 6 to 7 servings

Ingredients

1 cup pecans

1 teaspoon salt

1 ½ cup all-purpose baking mix

½ teaspoon pepper

2 packages of frozen whole okra (10.oz)

Peanut oil for frying

Directions

1. In a shallow pan, spread pecans in an single layer
2. Bake at 350°F for 10 minutes, until they are lightly toasted, stirring occasionally.
3. Process pecans, baking mix, salt, and pepper in a food processer until the pecans are finely ground.

4. In a large bowl, toss the okra and the pecan mixture to coat.

5. Pour oil into a Dutch oven, heating it to 350°F.

6. Fry the okra in batches until they are golden brown, 5 to 6 minutes

7. Drain on paper towels and serve.

Fried Confetti Corn

This yummy side dish is sure to have you asking for seconds. Simply nestle this dish next to a plate of greens to enjoy a healthy, heartwarming meal.

Makes 8 servings

Ingredients

6 cups fresh corn kernels

8 bacon slices

1 cup sweet onions, diced

½ cup green pepper, chopped

½ cup red pepper, chopped

1 package cream cheese (8 ounces)

1 teaspoon sugar

1 teaspoon salt

1 teaspoon pepper

½ cup half and half

Directions

1. In a large skillet, cook the bacon over medium high heat for 6 to 8 minutes until crispy.
2. Drain the bacon on paper towels, reserving about 2 tablespoons of drippings in the skillet. Coarsely crumble the bacon.

3. Sauté the corn, bell peppers and sweet onion over medium high heat for 6 minutes until tender.

4. Add cream cheese and half and half, stir the mixture until the cheese melts.

5. Stir in the sugar, salt, and pepper.

6. Transfer to a serving dish, and top with bacon.

Macaroni and Cheese

Serves 6-8

Ingredients

8 ounces dried elbow macaroni (you can also use whole wheat pasta if desired)
1/2 cup bread crumbs
¾ cups whole milk
¼ cup all-purpose flour
¼ cup butter, melted
1 cup sharp cheddar cheese + ½ cup for topping, shredded
1 cup Monterey jack cheese, shredded
1 cup processed cheddar cheese, cut into small cubes
1 pinch cayenne pepper
½ teaspoon paprika
Kosher salt and freshly ground pepper
Butter

Directions

1. Pre-heat the oven to 350°F.
2. Bring large pot of water to boil, add salt and cook pasta according to package instructions. Drain the macaroni in a strainer. Rinse under cold running water and drain to stop the cooking process.
3. Toss bread crumbs and melted butter to coat. Set aside
4. Generously butter a baking dish.
5. In a large mixing bowl, add all the ingredients EXCEPT the bread crumb mixture, and stir to combine. Transfer to the buttered casserole baking dish. Top with the bread crumbs mixture and cheddar cheese.
6. Place baking dish on baking sheet. Bake until bubbling, and cheesy top is golden brown, about 40-45 minutes. Let cool 5 minutes before serving.

Desserts

Strawberry Shortcake

It is hard to resist those bright colored gems and this cake is no different. In fact, this classic dessert is a big favorite in Southern cuisine. Full of fruity flavors, this dish will be a huge hit with the crowd.

Makes 8-12 servings

Ingredients

2 pounds fresh strawberries, hulled and quartered

¾ cup sugar, divided

¾ cup cold butter

2 large eggs

1 cup whipping cream

¼ teaspoon almond extract

1 container sour cream (8 ounces)

1 teaspoon vanilla extract

4 teaspoon baking powder

2 ¾ cups all-purpose flour

2 tablespoons sugar

Directions

1. Combine together the strawberries, ½ cup sugar, and almond extract. Cover the mixture and allow it to rest for 10 minutes.

2. At a medium speed, beat the whipping cream with an electric mixture until foamy.

3. Slowly add 2 tablespoons of sugar, beating until soft peaks start to form. Cover the mixture and keep refrigerated until ready to use.

4. Preheat the oven to 450°F.

5. Combine together the flour, remaining ¼ cup sugar and baking powder in a large bowl. Cut the butter into the flour mixture with pastry blender until crumbly.

6. In another bowl, whisk together sour cream, eggs, and vanilla until well blended, then add to the flour mixture and stir until all the dry ingredients are moistened.

7. Drop dough by lightly greased ⅓ cupfuls onto a lightly greased baking sheet, and bake for 12 to 15 minutes until golden.

8. Cut the shortcakes in half horizontally, and spoon ½ cup of the berry mixture and scoop it on the bottom of the short cake, top with a tablespoon of whipped cream, cover the top and serve with the remaining whipped cream.

Key Lime Pie

This delectable dessert is especially famous in Key West. You will be surprised how easy it is to make. If you love having something tangy, sweet, and creamy after your meals, this lime pie recipe is for you!

Makes 1 pie - 8 servings

Ingredients

Crust
¼ cup firmly packed light brown sugar

1 ¼ cups graham cracker crumbs

⅓ cup butter, melted

Filling
14 oz. can sweetened condensed milk

⅔ fresh lime juice

2 teaspoons lime zest

3 egg yolks

Topping
2 egg whites, at room temperature

2 tablespoon granulated sugar

¼ teaspoon cream of tartar

Directions

1. Preheat the oven at 350°F and place oven rack in middle position.

2. Combine the cracker crumbs, brown sugar, and melted butter in a 9 inch pie plate and press gently to form a crust.

3. Bake for 10 to 15 minutes until it is lightly brown, allow it to cool.

4. Beat the egg yolks until fluffy and light yellow in color, about 4-5 minutes on high speed. Slowly add the condensed milk, lime juice, and lime zest. Beat until fluffy, about 4-5 more minutes.

5. Pour filling in cooled graham crust. Set aside.

6. With an electric mixer, beat the egg whites and cream of tartar at high speed until foamy.

7. Gradually add the granulated sugar, 1 tablespoon at a time, and beat the mixture until soft peaks start to appear and the sugar is all dissolved.

8. Spread this meringue over the prepared pie filling.

9. Bake the pie into the oven at 325°F for 25 to 28 minutes.

10. Let cool down and place in the refrigerator 2-3 hours before serving.

Note: using key limes for the lime juice gives this pie an authentic flavor like no others.

Peach Ice Cream

This 6–ingredient, easy to make dessert will be a hit at home. Don't be surprised if your family and guests keep asking for this amazing chilly treat over and over again.

Makes 24 servings

Ingredients

4 cups peeled peaches, diced

1 cup sugar

1 can sweetened condensed milk (14 ounce)

1 package vanilla instant pudding mix (3.75 ounce)

1 can evaporated milk (12 ounce)

4 cups half and half

Directions

1. Combine the peaches and sugar together, and let stand for an hour.
2. Process in a food processor until smooth.
3. In a large bowl, stir together the evaporated milk and pudding mix, then add the peach puree, half and half, and condensed milk
4. Pour this mixture into an ice cream maker, and follow the manufacturer's instructions.

Bourbon Pecan Pie

This delectable bourbon dessert is something you will not be able to forget for a long time.

Makes 1 pie – 8-10 servings

Ingredients

½ cup sugar

½ cup light corn syrup

3 tablespoons butter, melted

½ cup brown sugar

2 cups pecan halves

2 tablespoons bourbon

3 eggs, beaten

1 deep dish pie crust (9 inch)

Directions

1. Preheat the oven to 375°F.
2. In a large bowl, mix together the white sugar, brown sugar, and butter together. Stir in the eggs, corn syrup and bourbon, and fold in the pecan halves.
3. Pour the filling into the deep dish pie crust.
4. Bake the pie in the preheated oven for 10 minutes, then reduce the heat to 350°F.
5. Continue to bake the pie for 25 minutes until the pie has set.
6. Cool on a cooling rack.

Coconut Layered Cake

Be ready to hit cake heaven with these layers of tropical coconut and soft whipped cream. This recipe is sure to become a favorite with the crowd at any time of the year.

Makes 8-12 servings

Ingredients

3 cups all-purpose flour

2 2/3 cups sugar

5 large eggs

1 package frozen flaked coconut (6 ounces)

1 ½ cups butter, softened

1 teaspoon vanilla extract

½ teaspoon salt

1 cup milk

1 teaspoon baking powder

1 cup coconut shavings

2 teaspoon baking powder

Coconut Filling

¼ cup powdered sugar

2 cups whipping cream

½ cup coconut flakes

1 teaspoon coconut extract

1 teaspoon vanilla extract

Directions

1. Preheat the oven to 400°F.
2. Beat the flour, sugar, butter, milk, baking powder, and salt together at medium speed with an electric mixer until well blended.
3. Add the extracts and blend well.
4. Gradually start adding the eggs, one at a time, beating until all the ingredients are blended.
5. Stir in the flaked coconut, and pour the batter in to 4 individual cake pans.
6. Bake the cakes for 20 minutes, and then cool on wire racks 10 minutes before removing them from the pans.
7. Reduce the oven temperature to 350°F and bake the coconut shavings in a single layer in a shallow pan, for 10 minutes or until toasted, stirring occasionally. Set the toasted coconut aside.
8. Beat whipping cream on high speed until foamy, and slowly add the coconut and vanilla extracts, coconut flakes and powdered sugar, beating the mixture until soft peaks start to foam.
9. When the cakes have cooled, prepare the coconut filling and spread it between the layers.
10. Spread the remaining frosting on the top and sides of the cake, and carefully press toasted coconut into the frosting.
11. Keep chilled until ready to serve.

Red Velvet Cake

Unsure about what sweet something you should try? This is a delicious dessert you've got to create in your kitchen. Bring the traditional Southern flavors home with this dessert.

Makes 8-12 servings

Ingredients

2 teaspoons fine salt

2 ¾ cups plus 1 tablespoon sifted cake flour

2 teaspoons baking powder

2 tablespoons red food coloring

¼ teaspoon baking soda

1 ½ tablespoons water

2 sticks unsalted butter, softened, plus some more for greasing pans

1 ½ teaspoons vanilla extract

2 cups granulated sugar

¼ cup unsweetened cocoa powder

3 large eggs

1 tablespoon finely grated orange zest

1 cup whole or low fat buttermilk

For Icing

1 pound sifted powdered sugar (4 cups)

1 ½ sticks unsalted butter (¾ cup)

1 pound cream cheese

2 tablespoons whole milk

Directions

1. Heat the oven to 350°F, and grease a 9 inch cake pan with butter, then flour. Tap off the excess flour, and set aside.
2. Sift the baking powder, baking soda, flour, and salt twice together, set aside.
3. Whisk the water, cocoa, vanilla, and food coloring in a small bowl until smooth, set aside.
4. In a large bowl, beat the butter on medium speed with an electric mixer until creamy, about 30 seconds. Add the sugar, ¼ cup at a time, beating about 15 minutes, until the mixture becomes fluffy.
5. Gradually add the eggs one at a time, along with the orange zest, beating after each addition. Add the red cocoa mix.
6. On low speed, alternately add the flour mixture and the buttermilk, starting and ending with the flour mixture. Beat the batter using a spatula, 10 to 12 strokes.
7. Divide cake batter into two cake pans, and bake for 30 minutes, or until a toothpick inserted in the center comes out clean.
8. Remove the cakes from the oven and allow the cakes to rest for 10 minutes before removing from the pans.
9. In the meantime, prepare the icing. In a large bowl, mix all the ingredients together at high speed, gradually reduce the speed until light and fluffy.
10. When the cakes are completely cool, place 1 cake on a serving plate. Spread the icing on the top. Place second cake on top and spread icing on top and sides.

Mississippi Mud Pie

We've saved the best for last. If you think fussy desserts are no good, you need to think again. Mississippi's favorite mud pie is going to have you wanting seconds...and thirds! This mud pie is going to be every dessert lover's dream.

Makes 1 pie - 8-12 servings

Ingredients

¼ cup sugar

1 package cream cheese (8 ounces)

¾ cup sugar

2 cups graham cracker crumbs

3 cups milk

1 package instant chocolate pudding mix (3 ½ ounce)

1 package instant butter scotch pudding mix (3 ½ ounce)

1 container whipped topping

Directions

1. Combine together the graham cracker crumbs with ¼ cup sugar and butter, and press firmly into a large pie plate.
2. Blend the cream cheese and sugar until smooth, and spread on the prepared crust.

97

3. In a separate bowl, mix together the pudding mixes and the milk until well blended and spread this on top of the cream cheese mixture.

4. Top with whipped topping.

5. Chill the pie.

Recipe Index

More Books by Louise Davidson

Here are some of Louise Davidson's other cookbooks.

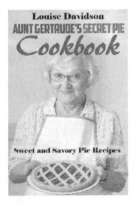

Appendix – Cooking Conversion Charts

1. Measuring Equivalent Chart

Type	Imperial	Imperial	Metric
Weight	1 dry ounce		28g
	1 pound	16 dry ounces	0.45 kg
Volume	1 teaspoon		5 ml
	1 dessert spoon	2 teaspoons	10 ml
	1 tablespoon	3 teaspoons	15 ml
	1 Australian tablespoon	4 teaspoons	20 ml
	1 fluid ounce	2 tablespoons	30 ml
	1 cup	16 tablespoons	240 ml
	1 cup	8 fluid ounces	240 ml
	1 pint	2 cups	470 ml
	1 quart	2 pints	0.95 l
	1 gallon	4 quarts	3.8 l
Length	1 inch		2.54 cm

* Numbers are rounded to the closest equivalent

2. Oven Temperature Equivalent Chart

Fahrenheit (°F)	Celsius (°C)	Gas Mark
220	100	
225	110	1/4
250	120	1/2
275	140	1
300	150	2
325	160	3
350	180	4
375	190	5
400	200	6
425	220	7
450	230	8
475	250	9
500	260	

* Celsius (°C) = T (°F)-32] * 5/9

** Fahrenheit (°F) = T (°C) * 9/5 + 32

*** Numbers are rounded to the closest equivalent

Made in the USA
Las Vegas, NV
09 March 2024

86967610R00066